IT'S WORK, BUT

IT'S WORTH IT!

Experiencing God's Best for Your Marriage

By Joseph Bryant, Jr.

xulon PRESS

It's Work, But It's Worth It
by Pastor Joseph Bryant Jr.

Printed in the United States of America

ISBN 1-60034-396-1

www.xulonpress.com

I BELIEVE IN YOUR MARRIAGE!

These are the words I share with every couple that comes to my office looking forward to their wedding day. I also share this encouragement with couples that are experiencing difficult days in their marriage, reminding them that THERE IS STILL HOPE. In a society that is continuously and aggressively opposed to God's biblical blueprint for marriage, with couples struggling to remain peaceful and joyful while making mountains out of molehills, with individuals so selfish they never embrace the idea that "two become one" because they are fighting for "what's mine is mine"—**SOMEBODY'S GOT TO BELIEVE IN MARRIAGE** – *God's wonderful plan for marital success!* Simply put IT'S WORK, **BUT IT'S WORTH IT!**

This study guide and the materials therein are morsels of information and inspiration to help couples WORK ON a marriage that is truly WORTH IT. The exercises and exhortations shared here come from over seventeen years of marital counseling, particularly the last ten years as a senior pastor, in which we have attempted to construct and reconstruct healthy relationships. Over and over, God has used these teachings to assist in the repairing, retooling, and rejuvenating of couples in their lifelong commitments to one another. My hope is that every person who picks up this resource will decide their marriage is WORTH THE WORK. None of us are perfect, and we all married imperfect people. Yet there is a "perfection" that is attained when two lives are intertwined to meet the needs of one another, build up one another, and complete one another in ways that could not have been accomplished as a single person. **God's plan for marriage still works**! God's blueprint for marriage is still the best! God's power for marriage is still available!

May this manual bless your life in reading it as much as it has blessed mine in sharing it. May the Lord bless all of you with the incredible marriage He wants you to enjoy!

IT'S WORTH IT!

Pastor Joseph Bryant, Jr.

DEDICATION

This work is dedicated to my beautiful wife, Kelly, who makes my life so precious! You are an incredible woman and an awesome wife, yet words cannot begin to describe what you mean to me.

I am so incredibly grateful for you, and I'm so happy to be married to you. You have truly made my life full and complete. I wouldn't be who I am without you - nor would I want to experience this journey without you!

—I ADORE YOU

ACKNOWLEDGMENTS

To my wonderful parents, Deacon and Mrs. Joseph Bryant, Sr., for giving me life and always encouraging my life. Thank you for showing me the value of staying together and knowing that it TAKES WORK but it is well WORTH IT. Your forty-plus years of marriage are an awesome testimony.

To my children, Josiah and Joi, thank you for giving me so much happiness and making me look forward to coming home!

To my friends and mentors, Dr. Alvin C. Bernstine and Dr. Larry W. Ellis, who have shaped all that I am in manhood, ministry, and marriage. I'm forever indebted to you.

To the GOOD NEWS TODAY Team, thanks for pushing me to write, and for supporting the ministry so sacrificially.

To the Marriage Ministry of Calvary Hill, thank you for allowing me the privilege of sharing the joys of the journey with you.

To the Ministerial Couples of Calvary Hill, thank you for opening your lives to me and for reminding me of how much marriage is truly WORTH IT!

To the Calvary Hill Community Church, YOU ARE THE BEST CHURCH IN THE WORLD! Thank you for letting me learn "on the job" how to be a pastor. I LOVE YOU!

HANDBOOK CONTENTS

SECTION ONE: Study Guide
Believing in God's Blueprint for Marriage

SECTION TWO: Fix-It-Kit
Confronting Marital Conflicts

SECTION THREE:
Happily Ever After...

Advice for the Road Ahead – Choosing to live in Harmony

IT'S WORK, BUT IT'S WORTH IT!

SECTION ONE: Study Guide

Believing in God's Blueprint for Marriage

TO HAVE AND TO HOLD

<u>The Blessing of Marriage</u>
Genesis 2:18-25

MARRIAGE IS THE GREATEST INSTITUTION IN THE WORLD!

Our wonderful God has designed a place for us to have constant companionship, intimate involvement, steady support, and practical partnership through the wonderful union called *marriage.* It is through this blessed relationship that God has planned for us to experience the joys of life together, to create life together, to encourage through life's tough times together, and to know that we are not living life alone – WE ARE TOGETHER. What an incredible reality **to have**; what a precious gift **to hold**.

As with all of God's plans for His people, He has given us a BLUEPRINT that gives us the structure for living out His awesome plan. In the beginning of His great book, the Bible, we find the account of God completing His week of creation by placing mankind into its appropriate place on this people planet called earth. Here He shares His heart for this jewel of creation and gives mankind a play-by-play description of how and why He designed the marriage institution (Gen. 2:18). **God did not want us to be alone, He wanted us to have a permanent partner:** *To have and to Hold.*

That is why the charge **"to have and to hold"** which is often given during the marriage ceremony is a cornerstone of the marriage covenant. The Lord's blueprint is most successful when this phrase enlists the best elements of relationships: commitment, passion, integrity, trust, intimacy, value… just to name a few.

THE BIBLICAL TEXT GIVES US A GREAT PICTURE OF WHAT "To Have and To Hold" looks like:

GOD'S BLUEPRINT FOR MARRIAGE PROVIDES:

_____ – *"It is not good that man be alone… make a suitable helper"* (v. 18)

_____ – *"She shall be called woman, for she was taken out of man"* (v. 23)

_____– *"For this reason a man will leave... and cleave" (v. 24)*

_____– *"The two were naked... and not ashamed" (v. 25)*

TO HAVE AND TO HOLD

<u>LOVE LESSONS</u>
Genesis 2:18-25

SUPPORT –
"It is not good that man be alone, I will make a <u>suitable helper</u> for him" (one who compliments/fits my life well; puzzle pieces)

_____

_____

_____

STRENGTH –
"She shall be called woman, for she was <u>taken out</u> of man" (you provide something for me, I'm a blessing to you)

_____

_____

_____

SECURITY –

"For this reason a man will <u>leave… and cleave</u>"
(I'm depending on you, you can depend on me- we're in this together)

_____

_____

_____

SAFETY –

"The two were naked and <u>not ashamed</u>" *(I give you all of me; I trust you with all of who I am – I love you for all that you are)*

_____

_____

_____

TO HAVE AND TO HOLD

STUDY REVIEW
Genesis 2:18-25

WHAT DOES THE TEXT SAY ABOUT MARRIAGE?

_____

_____

_____

WHAT DOES IT SAY TO THE MAN?

_____

_____

_____

WHAT DOES IT SAY TO THE WOMAN?

_____

_____

_____

WHAT CAN WE DO TO "MAKE IT WORK" THIS WAY?

_____

_____

_____

LOVER'S LANES

Understanding Our Roles in the Relationship

Ephesians 5:21-6:4

"Collisions on the road are the result of someone driving in another person's lane. If you want to be safe and successful, STAY IN YOUR LANE – and drive well"
- Anonymous

It is very difficult to have a successful **ride** in marriage if a husband and wife are confused about which "lane" each of them is to travel on. Therefore, it becomes extremely important for each person to understand the specific ROLE that God has given to them. Our Lord in His wisdom has defined "rules for the road" that help identify the role of a wife and the role of a husband. Once these roles are understood, it provides the framework for maximum fulfillment and love in the marital journey—in THE LOVER'S LANE.

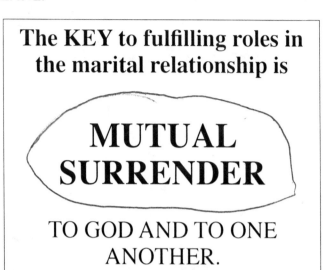

The KEY to fulfilling roles in the marital relationship is

MUTUAL SURRENDER

TO GOD AND TO ONE ANOTHER.

"Place yourselves under each other's authority out of respect for Christ" – Eph. 5:21

Then, and only then, can the marital roles be appropriately fulfilled. Without surrendering to God, we will fight His purpose and plan for our position in marriage. Without surrendering to our mate, we will not be able to contribute to the relationship what is needed to keep it strong and balanced.

MEN ARE CALLED TO SACRIFICE

WOMEN ARE CALLED TO SUBMIT

*A godly woman will choose to ___SACRIFICE___, **IF**
her husband is a man who will ___SUBMIT___
and do whatever it takes for the good of the family.*

*A godly man will choose to ~~SUBMIT~~ LEAD ___, **IF**
his wife is a woman who will ___SACRIFICE___ and
respect his godly leadership for the family.*

LOVER'S LANES

LOVE LESSONS
Ephesians 5:21-6:4

1)   *NEEDS MUST BE MET - verses 28- 29*

_____

_____

_____

2)   *NEVER CREATE DISTANCE - verse 31*

_____

_____

_____

3)   *NOTICE GOD'S EXAMPLE - verse 32*

_____

_____

_____

4) *NURTURE TAKES TIME - verse 33*

_____

_____

_____

LOVER'S LANES

STUDY REVIEW
Ephesians 5:21-6:4

WHAT DOES THE TEXT SAY ABOUT MARRIAGE?

_____

_____

_____

WHAT DOES IT SAY TO THE MAN?

_____

_____

_____

WHAT DOES IT SAY TO THE WOMAN?

_____

_____

_____

WHAT CAN WE DO TO "MAKE IT WORK" THIS WAY?

_____

_____

_____

WE ARE NOT "ALL" CREATED EQUAL!

*Genesis 1:26; 2:18-25 – Proverbs 5:15-23 –
Ephesians 5:22-6:4 – 1 Peter 3:1-7*

According to the creation account in Genesis 1, God created the human race with two distinct identities: male and female. From the beginning, God has given specific characteristics to each of the genders, although our world tries to erase the line of differentiation. In general, males and females have interesting characteristics that make each group "special", and these various traits make for wonderful experiences of growth and blessing in marriage. The differences between men and women should be celebrated and appreciated, for it is God Himself who made us in our own unique ways.

A FEW SIMPLE OBSERVATIONS...

Men were made from the DIRT – so they tend
to operate from the outside in
Women were made from inside the body close to
the HEART – so they tend to operate from
the inside out

Men as boys make nonverbal sounds when they
play - usually they often do so in the dirt
(non verbally with objects)
Women as girls make communication sounds when
they play - often with dolls (very verbal
and people oriented)

Men generally don't communicate their feelings
well (which is frustrating for women)
Women generally communicate their feelings *very*
well (which can be overwhelming to men)

Men generally try to let their INTELLECT guide
them in making choices
Women generally try to let their EMOTIONS guide
them in making choices

Men will often say "I think" when making
a statement
Women will often say "I feel" when making
a statement

Men were created EXTERNALLY MINDED, so
their values and conversations are connected to

things external, i.e. – their jobs, sports, politics, tools, cars, etc.
Women were created INTERNALLY MINDED, so their values and conversations are connected to things internal, i.e. – their children, people's feelings, emotional topics, family concerns

Men became MALES because of heightened testosterone in the womb; therefore, SEXUALLY:
Men are usually like microwave ovens
Women are usually like crock-pots

Men often *miss* what is obvious to women
Women often *dismiss* what is important to men

MEN DO NOT SEE THE WORLD LIKE WOMEN
WOMEN DO NOT SEE THE WORLD LIKE MEN

…AND THAT'S OKAY!

Don't expect your mate to be like you – love them for what God made them to be!

WE ARE NOT "ALL" CREATED EQUAL!

LOVE LESSONS

*Genesis 1:26; 2:18-25 – Proverbs 5:15-23 –
Ephesians 5:22-6:4 – 1 Peter 3:1-7*

BASIC NEEDS OF MEN

Affirmation

An attractive Wife

Domestic _____

*A Recreational
_____*

Sexual _____

BASIC NEEDS OF WOMEN

Security

A respectful Husband

Domestic _____

*A Spiritual
_____*

Relational _____

34

<u>HOW TO MEET THE NEEDS OF</u>

_____

_____

_____

_____

_____

LOVE LANGUAGES

Loving my mate where they need to be loved

Everyone loves to be loved, but not everyone receives love in the same way. What may be important to one person may not be so for another. The way one person feels valued and appreciated may be totally different from the way the very person they need validation and appreciation from practices those traits. It's remarkable how many people end up frustrated in marriage, either from assuming they are giving enough love or feeling that they are lacking in love received, simply because of a miscommunication in LOVE LANGUAGE.

LOVE LANGUAGES are the specific ways in which individuals receive love. Other modes may be understood, but only one or two really HIT THE SPOT and make us feel the necessary connection for marital intimacy and happiness. In a very unique way, we often end up in relationships with people who have a LOVE LANGUAGE that is **totally opposite of our own.** We therefore have to work that much harder to understand what our mate's needs are (since they are SO DIFFERENT from our own), and we have to spend more time explaining to our mate what needs we have ourselves.

*FIND YOUR LANGUAGE AND **SHARE IT** - LEARN THEIR LANGUAGE AND **DO IT!***

ACCEPTANCE
Your respect, your commitment, I know where you stand with me

ACTS OF SERVICE
Getting things done: chores, housework, "honey-dos," "baby-dos," etc.

AFFECTION
Physical touch: lots of hugs, holding, etc.

AFFIRMATION
Words or acts of validation; constant encouragement

APPRECIATION GIFTS
Stuff I can touch: presents, surprises, material things

ASSURANCE
Security: relational, emotional; I can be confident in you, I can trust you with me

AVAILABILITY

*Quality time; just being together -
pay attention to me*

LOVE LANGUAGES

Loving my mate where they need to be loved

LOVE LESSONS

<u>Never assume</u> that your mate knows what you
need, or knows how to give it to you.
Reveal your needs and remind your mate what
your "language" is regularly.
Don't be ashamed to teach them how to do it, or
ask for it to be done when it's not.
Don't take offense when your mate wants
to teach you how to love them in their
LANGUAGE.

"LOVE ISN'T LOVE UNTIL IT REACHES THE
ONE I LOVE!"

<u>**My love languages are:**</u>
1) _____ 2) _____ 3) _____

<u>**My mate's love languages are:**</u>
1) _____ 2) _____ 3) _____

HOW DO I MEET MY MATES LOVE LANGUAGE?

_____

_____

_____

_____

_____

IT'S WORK, BUT IT'S WORTH IT!

SECTION TWO: Fix-It-Kit

Confronting Marital Conflicts

MARRIED, BUT LIVING SINGLE

Genesis 2:18-25

MARRIAGE IS THE GREATEST INSTITUTION IN THE WORLD...

U nfortunately, many people are not enjoying the benefits of this great union because we don't realize one simple truth:

You did not get married to live alone! The "single life" is no longer the life that you live.

However, You MAY BE "living single"…:
- *If you can go a whole day without talking to one another and it doesn't cross your mind*
- *If you can be in the same house without enjoying each other's company or prefer to be in another room altogether*

- *If you can go weeks or months without having quality time together and you don't miss it*
- *If you consistently choose to work extra hours rather than spend time with your spouse*
- *If you regularly make plans for yourself (and your children) without consulting or considering your spouse*
- *If you have things in your life that you do not share or that are "off limits" to your spouse*
- *If you consistently look for opportunities to "leave your spouse" at home when you go where you go*
- *If you talk <u>to</u> and <u>about</u> your mate like an annoying acquaintance more than a precious partner*
- *If you assume what your spouse may do or think, react in anger or frustration, and never give them a chance to share their true feelings*
- *If you routinely share more about yourself (your goals, dreams, desires, pains, fears) with friends, coworkers, church members, and others than you share with your spouse*
- *If you still use the words **me**, **my**, and **mine** more than **we**, **us**, and **ours***

WHY BE MARRIED IF ONE CANNOT ENJOY THE BENEFITS OF PARTNERSHIP?

(Why own stock in something you can't reap benefits from?)

**HOW CAN <u>TWO</u> ENJOY BEING <u>ONE</u>
IF <u>ONE</u> OF THE TWO REFUSES
TO ACT AS <u>ONE</u>?**

*A lack of intimacy, investment, and involvement
with your mate will rob you both.*

MARRIAGE TAKES WORK – BUT IT'S WORTH IT!

REALITY CHECKS:
- Pain creates distance, unresolved pain creates discord
- Avoiding a conflict only increases the conflict
- Not talking is NOT optional, all talking is not necessary

If your marriage is not what God intended, at least half of your life is out of order, and the other half is miserable.

TAKE TIME TO MAKE TIME
- Once a week have a "simple" date
  (dinner & a movie, lunch & a walk, long drive & a snack, etc.)

- ## Once a month do a "special" date
  (something planned ahead; something to look
  forward to – concert/sporting event, dress-up dinner,
  double date, someone's "favorites": food, thing to do,
  place to go, etc.)

- ## Once a quarter do something EXTRA special (beach/sightseeing, overnighter/getaway, etc.)

- ## Once a year, go away together, renew your commitments.
  (Ask what THEY need, share what YOU need – talk
  about where your life IS and where your life is
  GOING.)

WORK IT OUT!

Doing what it takes to create a peaceful, positive, and pleasing marriage

FOUR MAJOR AREAS OF COUPLE CONFLICT AND MARITAL MADNESS:

1)   UNRESOLVED PAST PAIN
     (In the relationship, past relationships, or from one's upbringing)

2)   UNRECEIVED LOVE LANGUAGE
     (I'm not being loved in the way I need to be loved)

3) ## UNCLEAR COMMUNICATION
(We aren't talking, and when we do, we aren't listening)

4) ## UNCLEAR, UNMET, OR UNREALISTIC EXPECTATIONS
(This is not what I wanted in my marriage; I thought I had one thing, but...)

DIAGNOSIS – "What is the issue?"

UNRESOLVED PAST PAIN
Confession – why am I like this?
Correction – what do **I need to do** to get over this?

UNRECEIVED LOVE LANGUAGE
What do I need most from my mate?
What do I need to do most for my mate?

UNCLEAR COMMUNICATION
Have I listened to their heart?
Do we talk WITH each other, or do we talk AT each other?
NOT TALKING IS NOT OPTIONAL

UNCLEAR, UNMET, OR UNREALISTIC EXPECTATIONS

I came into this with blinders on
I didn't want to see what I saw
I wanted something that I knew wasn't there
then, and still isn't there now
I thought they would change, I thought I
could change them
I thought things would be easier once we got
married

Never STOP DATING!!

WORK IT OUT! (Pt. 2)
Doing what it takes to create a peaceful, positive, and pleasing marriage

PROGNOSIS – "How do we get it right NOW?"

SUGGESTED REMEDIES:

Address UNRESOLVED PAST PAIN

- **FORGIVE AND FORGIVE**
  (Stop counting and recounting, and let it go - Matt. 18:22)
- **GET OVER IT FAST**
  (Never let an unaddressed pain live longer than a day – Eph. 4:26)
- **GET HELP IF NEEDED**
  (Seek godly, healthy help - Prov. 11:14)
- **DON'T HOLD YOUR MATE HOSTAGE ANYMORE**
  (**CHOOSE** TO BE HAPPY TOGETHER! – Eph. 33)

Ask for UNRECEIVED LOVE LANGUAGE

- Figure out what you need. Tell your mate.
- Find out what they need. DO THAT – over and over – and do it well!

- DON'T WAIT UNTIL THEY DO THEIR PART BEFORE YOU DO YOURS
- BE **THE BEST** AT WHAT YOUR MATE WANTS AND NEEDS FROM YOU
  (Never leave them lacking)

Attempt to improve UNCLEAR COMMUNICATION

- MAKE NO ASSUMPTIONS (assumptions kill relationships)
- RECEIVE, REPEAT, RESPOND (make sure you understand your mate before you react to what they say)
- Take 15 minutes to share your day with each other
- Take 5 minutes to pray together daily for the both of you
- Take 1 minute to check in each day when you're apart

Re-Arrange UNCLEAR, UNMET, OR UNREALISTIC EXPECTATIONS

- MAKE YOUR MARRIAGE YOUR PRIORITY
  (Think: how can **I** bless our marriage today? How can **I** make this a better relationship?)
- ACCEPT WHO YOU MARRIED (don't try to change them, let <u>your</u> heart and <u>God's</u> hand do it!)

- UNDERSTAND **YOUR** ROLE ACCORDING TO **GOD'S WORD** (see page #)
- PRAY THAT GOD LETS YOU SEE THE BEST IN YOUR MATE ALWAYS
- NEVER, EVER ATTACK YOUR MATE (physically, verbally, emotionally), IN PERSON OR OTHERWISE
- ASK GOD TO CHANGE **YOU** INSTEAD OF ASKING HIM TO CHANGE THEM
- ADMIT YOUR OWN FAULTS BEFORE ACKNOWLEDGING THEIR FAULTS
- DON'T GET DISTRACTED (in thoughts, words, actions, etc. – buried in work, kids, church, other)
- TEACH YOUR MATE HOW TO LOVE YOU

MOST OF ALL, <u>PRAY, PRAY, AND PRAY</u> SOME MORE THAT GOD WOULD HEAL THE HURTS OF YOUR PAST, HELP YOU TO FORGIVE PAST PROBLEMS, AND EMBRACE THE PLACE THAT HE WANTS TO TAKE YOU <u>NOW!</u>

7 STEPS IN 7 DAYS TO BEGIN RELATIONSHIP RESTORATION

(For those in critical care)

These recommendations are specially designed for couples that are experiencing a time of conflict, distance, disappointment, and despair in their marriage. **THIS IS A 7-DAY EXERCISE that must be fully committed to by both mates.** Each of the 7 steps is critical to the process, and must be carried out with intention and consistency. May these tools assist you in restoring your marriage to the beautiful relationship God intended you both to have!

7 STEPS (Instructions)

1) No complaints – only compliments *(Stop bickering and start blessing)*

2) No smart remarks – only sweet reminders *(Watch what you say and how you say it)*

3) Pray together in the morning – read the bible together at night *(Make God the center of your marriage)*

4) Call once a day to share your love *(Just called to say I love you)* – call once a day to share your day

5) Make love on the first day – make love on the last day *(Rekindle the fire of passion)*

6) Have one dream date for him – have one dream date for her *(Do something special for each one)*

7) Agree to give your best – ask God to do the rest *(It's Work, But It's Worth It)*

*NOTE: If any item is broken, you must start over again with Day One

PREREQUISITES:

Prior to beginning this exercise, write a short paragraph describing your feelings on the following subjects:

YOUR SPOUSE
YOUR FEELINGS
YOUR FAITH
YOUR BELIEF IN MARRIAGE

Write a prayer to God about what you want Him to do in YOU.

Ask another couple to pray for you before you begin and to be available to you throughout the seven days for accountability, support, encouragement, assistance, etc. (This should be a couple you trust, one that displays marital and spiritual strengths, and one in which both of you are comfortable with your spouse talking to)

THIS EXERCISE IS NOT MEANT TO UNCOVER OR ERASE THE REALITY OF DEEP-SEEDED ISSUES OF PAIN, BETRAYAL, DISTRUST, OR ABUSE. HOWEVER, THESE BEHAVIORS, WHEN COMMITTED TO, CAN CREATE THE POSITIVE ENVIRONMENT, EMOTIONS, AND EXPERIENCES THAT CAN REKINDLE, RECONNECT, AND REFRESH YOUR RELATIONSHIP IN SUCH A WAY THAT YOU BEGIN TO JOURNEY DOWN THE PATH TO WHOLENESS, HEALTH, AND HAPPINESS!

IT'S WORK,
BUT IT'S WORTH IT!

SECTION THREE: Happily Ever After…

Advice for the Road Ahead – Choosing to live in Harmony

12 MOST IMPORTANT WORDS IN MARRIAGE...

I WAS WRONG

I AM SORRY

PLEASE FORGIVE ME

I LOVE YOU

Use these regularly: *THEY WILL SAVE YOUR MARRIAGE!*

SAYINGS AND STUFF

Don't sweat the small stuff.

Your mate is not that bad, look who they married!

Keep your marriage SAFE – always let your mate be himself or herself.

Never judge their emotions, no matter how CRAZY they seem to you.

Don't let others dictate how you feel about your mate.

Remember the good times.

Never stop dating.

Be the best mate you can be, every day!

IT TAKES WORK, BUT IT'S WORTH IT!

Summaries & Scriptures

GOD CREATED MEN TO BE FAMILY
LEADERS: protector and provider for the
family (Gen. 2).

*A GOOD MAN LEADS BEST BY LISTENING
CAREFULLY TO HIS WIFE (1 Pet. 3:7).*

GOD CREATED WOMEN TO BE FAMILY
NURTURERS: caregivers, emotional
strength. (Titus 2)

*A GOOD WOMAN NURTURES BEST BY
KNOWING HOW TO TAKE CARE OF THE
NEEDS OF HER MATE, HER CHILDREN, AND
HERSELF WELL (Prov. 31:10-31).*

EVERY MAN **NEEDS**
ENCOURAGEMENT, VALIDATION, AND
SUPPORT FROM HIS WIFE

EVERY WOMAN **NEEDS** SECURITY, RESPECT, AND TO BE VALUED BY HER HUSBAND
Just Do It!

COMPROMISE ISN'T ALWAYS 50/50:
It's usually whatever needs to be done to keep PEACE!

WE ALL NEED GOOD EXAMPLES OF GODLY MARRIAGE.
*FIND ONE **OR** BECOME ONE.*

DON'T LET OUTSIDE FORCES DETERMINE WHAT KIND OF COUPLE YOU ARE, OR WHAT KIND OF MARRIAGE YOU SHOULD HAVE.

NEVER TAKE ADVICE FROM THOSE WHO ARE BITTER.

CONFLICT IS GOD'S REMINDER TO US OF OUR IMPERFECTIONS.
Remember, It's WORK but It's WORTH IT.

SPECIAL NOTE – FOR YOUR PROTECTION:

MOST AFFAIRS ARE NOT ABOUT SEX:

THEY ARE OFTEN THE BYPRODUCT OF SOMEONE'S NEEDS BEING IGNORED
(Not loved in their love language, unappreciated, devalued, lack of communication, etc.)
THEN AN OUTSIDER PROVIDES THE DESIRED ATTENTION IN A CONVENIENT WAY.

TO PROTECT YOUR MARRIAGE...
PRIORITIZE YOUR MATE'S NEEDS YOURSELF. NEVER LEAVE THEM LACKING THE THINGS THEY NEED FROM YOU THE MOST! IF THEIR NEEDS ARE SUPPLIED BY YOU, THERE IS MUCH LESS CHANCE FOR ANOTHER PERSON TO INTERFERE.

MARRIAGE TAKES WORK, BUT IT'S WORTH IT.

PRAYERS AND GOALS
for Our Marriage

_____

_____

_____

_____

_____

_____

_____

_____

_____

MARRIAGE PRAYER

*Lord, help us to remember
when we first met
and the strong love
that grew between us.
To work that love into
practical things so nothing
can divide us.*

*We ask for words both
kind and loving
And hearts always ready
to ask forgiveness
as well as forgive.*

*Dear Lord, we put our marriage
into Your hands.
Amen.*

Author Unknown

FACILITATOR'S NOTES
For Groups, Couples or Individual Studies

STUDY GUIDE "FILL IN'S"

TO HAVE AND TO HOLD

The Blessing of Marriage
Genesis 2:18-25

GOD'S BLUEPRINT FOR MARRIAGE PROVIDES:

SUPPORT   – *"It is not good that man be alone… make a suitable helper" (v. 18)*

STRENGTH   – *"She shall be called woman, for she was taken out of man" (v. 23)*

SECURITY   – *"For this reason a man will leave… and cleave" (v. 24)*

SAFETY   – *"The two were naked… and not ashamed" (v. 25)*

– –

LOVER'S LANES

Understanding Our Roles in the Relationship
Ephesians 5:21-6:4

MEN ARE CALLED TO **SACRIFICE**

WOMEN ARE CALLED TO **SUBMIT**

*A godly woman will choose to <u>SUBMIT</u>, **IF** her husband is a man who will <u>SACRIFICE</u> and do whatever it takes for the good of the family.*

*A godly man will choose to <u>SACRIFICE</u>, **IF** his wife is a woman who will <u>SUBMIT</u> and respect his godly leadership for the family.*

WE ARE NOT "ALL" CREATED EQUAL!

LOVE LESSONS
Genesis 1:26; 2:18-25 – Proverbs 5:15-23 – Ephesians 5:22-6:4 – 1 Peter 3:1-7

BASIC NEEDS OF MEN

Affirmation

*An **ATTRACTIVE** Wife*

*Domestic **SUPPORT CONCERN***

*A Recreational **PARTNER***

*Sexual **FULFILLMENT***

BASIC NEEDS OF WOMEN

Security

*A **RESPECTFUL** Husband*

Domestic

*A Spiritual **LEADER***

*Relational **INTIMACY***

Printed in the United States
62200LVS00001B/1-258